Abandonment

to

Forgiveness

Michelle Moore

Paige Henderson

Sharon Kay Ball

The Freedom Series
Created by Michelle Borquez

AspirePress

Torrance, California

Abandonment to Forgiveness

© Copyright 2013 God Crazy/Bella Publishing
Aspire Press, a division of Rose Publishing, Inc.
4733 Torrance Blvd., #259
Torrance, California 90503 USA
www.aspirepress.com

Register your book at www.aspirepress.com/register
Get inspiration via email, sign up at www.aspirepress.com

Contents

Chapter 1

Michelle's Story 5

Chapter 2

Bible Study 21

Chapter 3

Steps to Freedom 73

The Authors

Michelle Moore was abandoned by her parents as a young teen. She carried that bitterness like an abscess for many years. When she finally faced the pain and turned to the God who will never leave, she began a journey toward mercy, forgiveness, and healing.

Paige Henderson is sought after nationally and internationally as a speaker who loves unlocking the passion in the hearts of women. Paige and her husband, Richard, founded Fellowship of the Sword Ministries [www.fellowshipofthesword. com].

Sharon Kay Ball is a licensed professional counselor and a mother to three children. In addition to her private practice, Sharon is a staff counselor at her church. Her own personal experience with suffering, the daily grind of single parenting, and counseling her clients has given Sharon tremendous compassion and insight for those dealing with life's tragedies and trials.

Chapter 1

Michelle's Story

By Michelle Moore

"And forgive us our sins, for we also forgive
everyone who is indebted to us."
—Luke 11:4 (NKJV)

When I was fourteen, my mother changed her
identity and then left me. For nearly eighteen
years I didn't know if she was dead or alive.
This abandonment was the most painful thing
that ever happened to me, and it left its mark
for many years. Immediately after my mom left,
I became a shell of the girl I had been before.
Wracked by pain, fear, and emptiness, I did not

recognize my life at all. My mother and I had been so close. She and my dad were divorced, and Mom was my best friend. Then she left me. I couldn't call her. I couldn't write. I had no idea where she had gone or why.

I would lie in bed and say to myself, *Just how awful am I? Even the mothers of murderers and rapists visit their children in prison. My mother left me. Just up and left. How awful must I really be?* I would ponder over and over what I had done that could have been so bad, and I blamed myself for her decision. My self-esteem plummeted and all sorts of insecurities reared their ugly heads with a vengeance. My father wasn't much help either. After my mother left, my grandfather asked me to wait one month before I contacted my father. By the time that month had passed, I had already been sent to live with an aunt and uncle in another city. It was clear to me very quickly that their home was not a place I wished to remain. However, when I asked my father if I could live with him, he responded with talk of his having "a new family now" (referring to my stepmother and their three-month-old baby). He asked if I could just stay where I was. My own parents didn't want me. My aunt and uncle thought of me as a burden. How could anyone else want me?

Abandonment is ugly. I couldn't put that event in the back of my mind and act like it didn't matter. I could not pretend that it had never happened. After all, there were so many constant reminders of what I was missing— Mother's Day, family holidays. My friends had mothers. Moms were everywhere, except for mine.

The people around me could not understand or relate to the deep pain I carried. On the outside, I looked perfectly fine. On the inside, I was crying out for help. My feeling that no one

understood what I was going through left me
isolated and alone. I could be in a room filled
with people and feel like I was the loneliest
person in the world.

During the eighteen years that my mother was
gone, I struggled to make sense of her absence.
Eventually, I began to build my own life without
her. I grew
up, but every   I wished my mother
achievement,   was there with me.
every milestone
in my life, carried a dark cloud because my
mother wasn't there to witness it. My high
school graduation, my wedding, even the births
of my children were tainted by the absence
that had become more like an abscess in my
heart. When my youngest son Carson was
born, I cried—not tears of joy for his arrival,
but of despair because I wished my mother
was there with me. Because she had simply
disappeared from my life, I had no closure.
The "not knowing" brought on fear, worry,

and grief that words cannot fully describe. The void in my life and hole in my heart remained a festering wound.

I spent many years searching for the love, value, and hope I did not get from my mother and father. I tried to find value and worth at home, but they were not there. I thought I could find them in business. However, regardless of the successes, accolades, money, and material possessions I earned, I still couldn't find or replace what had been missing in my earlier years.

One night, like so many others, I found myself crying inconsolably to my husband about the injustices and hurts from my childhood and the pain of my parents' abandonment. Meanwhile our own children played in the next room. When I realized what I was doing, I felt convicted. I was ashamed. I was crying about the past while my loving husband, our adorable children, and I were safe and healthy in our beautiful home. I couldn't help but wonder how many mothers pray for healthy children every day, or pray for loving husbands, or wish they had a safe place to live. Here I was, letting life pass me by, not enjoying the blessings that the Lord had given me. Still, I hurt. I cried. I couldn't get past my past.

That night, as I cried, everything came to a head. I finally realized that the reason my pain wouldn't heal was because I had not forgiven my parents. I was still carrying the weight because I had not let go. Finally, I was forced to face my past. I had to confront the pain in order for healing to happen.

That was the first step in my healing. I began to understand that God was with me at all times, and that he was not going to leave me like my parents had. They may have abandoned me, but God never had. He was different. Upon realizing this fact, things began to change. For so long I had felt like I was a puzzle with pieces missing. But now, slowly, I was finding those pieces and putting each into their place. As my relationship grew with the Lord, my parents' shortcomings didn't matter so much. It wasn't the end of the world, as it had always felt like to me.

As I journeyed down the path, I slowly began to feel mercy, grace, and forgiveness in a way I never had before. I began to consider human nature, and I realized that sometimes when people make poor decisions they don't always know how deeply they wound others. My mother might have told herself that even at a young age, I was better off without her being in my life. My father might have believed that it was best to keep his distance from everyone involved—including me—in order to avoid confrontations with other family members. Truth be told, I may never know their reasons. But I wouldn't be the person I am today if it weren't for the choices—good and bad—that my parents made.

I share all of this because I want to encourage anyone holding forgiveness hostage to let it go. Avoid making the same mistakes I did. If we don't forgive others, it is impossible for us to heal. Although it is rewarding, forgiveness is a journey. It is one of the hardest things I have ever had to do in my life. It's not just something I said only once and it was done; I had to commit to it and recommit to it often.

I knew that, as a Christian, I must forgive. It is not a choice; it is a command. I had withheld forgiveness because I was waiting until my parents, who had wronged me, asked for forgiveness. This withholding helped me feel in control of the situation. But the Bible doesn't say we get to forgive when we have decided that a person has suffered enough—according to us—to atone for their actions. It says we must forgive. No ifs, ands, or buts.

It took time for me to realize that forgiveness doesn't mean the person has permission to hurt me again, nor does it mean that I will forget. It doesn't even mean that they will be so moved by my graciousness that they will change their behavior. I had to realize that, more than likely, the person who has offended and deeply hurt me has no idea how hurt I am. After all, they are not the one walking in my shoes. They may not even realize they hurt me in the first place.

It was like a switch had flipped. After so many years, I experienced a revelation. I realized that while I was wallowing in my pain, my mother and father had gone on with their lives, likely unaware of the damage they caused.

Forgiveness doesn't mean that everything will be fixed and relationships will be miraculously restored. But it does mean that we choose not to seek revenge or reciprocity. And by the way, if we put conditions or expectations on our forgiveness of others, we set ourselves up to be hurt again and again.

Forgiveness is a choice only you can make. Not just once, but over and over. To the man asking how many times he should forgive, Jesus said, "I do not say to you, up to seven times but, up to seventy times seven" (Matthew 18:22 NKJV). The depth of forgiveness Jesus taught is not about the size of numbers; it's about the size of your heart. Forgiveness is not always easy, but the rewards are limitless.

I had endured years upon years of anger, grief, horror, tears, fear, and suicidal depression. I had been dragging around a bag filled with pain and bad memories since the nightmare started. But I could not change what happened. The "what ifs" and "if onlys" were neither productive nor healthy. Instead, I had to make a conscious decision to take what happened and use it for good. God has moved in my life and I decided to share it with others. Amazingly, when I stopped focusing on myself and instead focused my time and energy on helping other people, my own healing began to grow by leaps and bounds.

My head had been swimming with angry questions for God: *Why did this happen to me? Why did the other person get to move on? What am I supposed to do with all this hurt?* Life is full of difficult questions like these that we can't possibly answer because we don't see all that God sees. But I decided to trust God. Now, he is already using the years of suffering to strengthen me and to glorify him, and he will continue to do so. I just had to take the first step.

Now imagine what happened when I discovered, after an eighteen-year absence, that my mother was alive and well in a distant state. One morning, I heard a voice on the phone that I didn't recognize announce herself as my mother. After some questioning to determine the authenticity of the call, my heart dared to hope that all would be well and I would get the answers I had needed for so long. After a face-to-face meeting and some interaction with my mom, I came to realize that my dreams of a sweet reunion, with everything lining up to fill the hole in my heart, were not to be a reality.

The true reason for her sudden return became apparent almost immediately. She was in great financial need and was looking for money. Yes, she was alive and that was great news. But she was oblivious of what she had done to me and how it wreaked havoc on my life. That oblivion, coupled with her not caring about the years she lost with me or about the news of being a grandmother, was the beginning of a painful realization that my mother had not missed me. She chose to be away all those years and had only returned when she thought it would benefit her financially. However, here is where the true blessing lies: I was deeply hurt—*but I had a choice*. I could stay hurt and be bitter or I could look healing in the face. Either way, I knew the work would have to start with me.

I found myself standing at the proverbial fork in the road. Which path did I want to go down? I could see that choosing the path of anger and pain would only lead me to living in the past. But by choosing to stand on God's promises, I could see it leading to true healing and happiness. So I chose to ask God for his help in finding closure. I asked God to lead the way to help me move on. He answered, and for that, I am grateful.

One of the best things I did was to commit to not making the same choices that had harmed me. My parents weren't around for me physically and emotionally. However, I chose to be the best mother I could possibly be. And I chose wisely when I married my husband. I saw his heart for children and knew I would be providing a great father for my future children. My husband says all the time how grateful he is that my childhood was the way it was. He says that he knows I am the great mother I am because of what I didn't have as a child.

Obedience to God begins with humility. We must believe that his way is better than our own. We may not always understand his ways of working, but by humbly obeying, we will receive his blessings. We must remember that God can use anything to accomplish his purposes. When you can remember what happened and direct those emotions toward doing something significant and positive today, you can declare yourself an overcomer.

This past Christmas Day, I was joyful. There was no anxiety about the upcoming holiday, with disappointing thoughts of another Christmas without my parents. During the build up to Christmas Day, no longer did I think, *Only a few more days until the day I will be crushed yet again.* This year there were no tears or feelings of sadness and emptiness. There was no longing for my parents and the childhood that had been stolen from me. Instead, I spent the day enjoying family and good food while thanking God that we were all together, happy, and healthy. Our home was filled with love, laughter, and joy. It wasn't until that evening, while cuddled up on the sofa with my boys, that I realized how happy I was, and just how happy I'd been all day.

You see, this year was different. This was the year that I chose to walk down the path marked *forgiveness* and learned how sweet it is with Jesus holding the lantern to light the way.

Bank accounts will go up and down. Jobs will come and go. People will disappoint you over and over again. But if you are able to forgive and have hope that today, tomorrow, and every day thereafter your best days are still to come, you have everything you need. *You can do all things through Christ who strengthens you* (Philippians 4:13 NKJV); and that includes forgiveness.

Abandonment to Forgiveness

Chapter 2

Bible Study

By Paige Henderson

Let Me Pour Us a Cup 'O Truth

I cannot think of many things more awful than being left. Abandonment—walking out the door without an explanation or a simple good-bye—is one of the ugliest and deepest forms of hurt. What do you do? How do you compute? To whom do you turn when the one who leaves you, like in Michelle's case, is your own *mother*? Mothers are our nurturers, teachers, and protectors who show us how to navigate a challenging world. They teach us what do in word and action. They help us figure out who we are as women. Your mother is the source of life well beyond the womb. What do you do when the nurturer and teacher is the one doing the abandoning? As Michelle's story illustrates, it wrecks your entire foundation of security and confidence and leaves you resentful.

How do you forgive that? Recall what Michelle said: "I was deeply hurt—*but I had a choice. I could stay hurt and be bitter or I could look healing in the face.*" The first step in healing is forgiving.

For Christ-followers, forgiveness is one of those spiritual disciplines that we all think is a great idea until we have to do it. And the deeper the cut, the harder it is to forgive. The forgiveness battle is waged on all fronts. Spiritually, you know that forgiveness is right, but you either don't want to do it or you can't see that there is a better life on the other side of this hurt. Emotionally, you fight against negative feelings—bitterness, resentment, anger, fear, rage—that bob to the surface at the most inopportune times. Physically, your body is experiencing a host of stress responses such as increased blood pressure, digestive issues, or immune system weakness that can result from preoccupation with the hurt and the gerbil-in-a-wheel need to keep moving while you try to salvage what's left of your life.

Forgiving is truly an issue of counting the cost and deciding, as Michelle did, that either you can stay bitter and deal with the totality of issues that come with that choice, or you can heal . . . and live! I would encourage you to take a similar journey toward healing. Pick up your backpack and let's go exploring in the fields of forgiveness!

What's the Big Deal About Forgiveness, Anyway?

From Michelle's Story

"[The] hole in my heart remained a festering wound."

So what's the big deal about forgiveness? You mean, other than potentially losing years off your life?! In addition to the physical implications, the spiritual implications of holding on to unforgiveness are enormous.

We're just beginning the discussion of forgiveness, but let's get some things clear. Right from the start, we must know what forgiveness is and what it isn't. Here is a list of myths about forgiveness that I've collected over the years while counseling people through the forgiveness process. All of these false ideas about forgiveness can block true forgiveness from our lives. If you find that one of these roadblocks is set up in your life right now, take a moment to pray about it, and then agree to reconsider your ideas when you hear what the Lord really has to say.

Myth #1: Forgiveness is a choice; therefore, unforgiveness is not a sin. I was the one offended and it is my right to be offended.

The Lord very clearly tells us to forgive. Look up in your Bible and read the following verses and answer the questions:

Matthew 6:14–15
What happens if you don't forgive?

_____

_____

_____

_____

_____

_____

Matthew 7:1–2

How is judgment toward you determined?

_____

_____

_____

_____

Mark 11:25–26

What comes as a result of your forgiveness?

_____

_____

_____

_____

Forgiveness is a choice. But just because it's a choice doesn't mean that if you choose not to do it, you're exempt from the consequences.

The choice not to forgive isn't like turning down a piece of chocolate cake or saying "no, thank you" to a movie invitation. The choice not to forgive is a choice whether or not to be obedient to what God has told you to do. Your unforgiveness is not an issue between you and the person who hurt you; it's between you and God.

Myth #2: Forgiveness restores a relationship, and I just can't do that right now. I'm not ready for any kind of relationship of any kind; truthfully, I don't want any kind of relationship with the person who hurt me.

Forgiveness is not reconciliation. Those are two different things. Sometimes they go together, but not always. Forgiveness is an issue between you and the Lord. Reconciliation is an issue between you and the other person. Withholding forgiveness produces consequences in your own heart and affects your relationship with God.

Not being reconciled to the person who hurt you has a different set of procedures altogether.

Forgiveness of others creates a clear path in your relationship with the Lord. Forgiveness is indeed very personal. But it's not personal between you and "them"; it's personal between you and God. Look at the following verses to see what harboring unforgiveness in your heart can do in your relationship with God.

James 4:17
According to James, if you don't do what's right, what is that called?

_____

_____

_____

_____

_____

What's the "right thing to do"? Whatever God tells you to do. You've already read what God's

Word says about forgiveness—and most of that
was words spoken directly by Jesus.

John 9:31
What do we know?

_____

_____

_____

_____

_____

There are two characteristics of the person
whom God hears. List those below.

1. _____

2. _____

John 15:7
The key to this verse is the part about abiding
(remaining) in Christ. The word *abide* means
to be or remain united in heart, mind, and will.
Consider all the verses that you've looked up so

far. What is Jesus telling you about forgiveness? Journal your thoughts and feelings.

_____

_____

_____

_____

_____

_____

_____

_____

_____

_____

_____

Myth #3: Before forgiveness can be given, true repentance must be shown on the part of the offender. They have to get it right and ask for forgiveness. If they aren't asking, I'm not giving! It's their responsibility to realize how much they hurt me.

Jesus forgave even while he was being crucified. Read the story of his crucifixion in **Luke 23:13–37**. Find the verse where Jesus forgives those who are crucifying him. Read a few verses before and after that verse. Then, locate the verse where the Jews or the Roman soldiers or the Roman citizens who attended the crucifixion asked for his forgiveness. Write it below.

_____

_____

_____

_____

It's not there. You didn't miss something. They didn't ask. But he gave.

Keeping this thought in mind, consider the story of Stephen in the book of Acts. In the early days of the first church in Jerusalem, the twelve disciples needed help in taking care of the growing number of Jesus' followers. The disciples selected seven men, including Stephen, to take over the ministry of serving meals to needy people, among other ministry duties. The work of these seven men would allow the disciples to devote their time to prayer and studying the Word. Some men from the local synagogue began to argue with Stephen. They falsely accused Stephen of speaking untruths about the law and for speaking against synagogue worship. His accusers even got people to lie and give false testimony against him. Stephen was brought before the high priest to defend himself against the false accusations, and he took the opportunity to tell them all about Jesus. At the end of his defense, the listeners were so mad they drove Stephen out of town and stoned him.

Read Acts 7:58–60. Stephen asks God to forgive the ones who were stoning him. Can you find the verse where they asked him to do that?

No, they didn't ask.

In neither the story of Stephen nor of Jesus on the cross did the people who were being forgiven show any remorse or repentance, nor did they stop and begin to reconcile. Forgiveness is not dependent on a change of heart from the person who hurt you. While that would be nice, and sometimes this happens, it isn't necessary. Forgiveness isn't about a change in them. Forgiveness is about a change in you.

Myth #4: The ability to forgive is a personality trait. Some people are just naturally more forgiving than others. I just don't have that type of personality.

Forgiveness is as much a spiritual discipline as is prayer. You learn it; you aren't born to it. When the disciples asked Jesus to teach them to pray in **Luke 11:1–4**, forgiveness was part of the lesson. Jesus gives them a sample—a model—of what a prayer looks like and what the regular contents of prayers should be.

First, honor God. *"Father, hallowed be Your name. Your kingdom come."*

Second, make requests. *"Give us each day our daily bread."*

Third, forgive. *"And forgive us our sins, for we ourselves also forgive everyone who is indebted to us."*

Fourth, submit to God's authority. *"And lead us not into temptation."*

These are clear instructions, given for all personality types to follow!

Myth #5: Forgiveness comes when justice has been satisfied. If you forgive someone prematurely, then the lesson God wants them to learn will be wasted. They'll just do this again because they'll think that mistreating me is okay.

This is really about revenge, isn't it? It's very hard to forgive if you fear that in so doing the other person will be "let off the hook," so to speak.

The first mention of forgiveness in the shadow of retaliation is in the story of Joseph, near the end of the book of Genesis. Joseph was the favored son of his father, Jacob, which made him the hated brother. His older brothers so hate him that they want to kill him. Instead, they sell him into slavery and tell their dad that he was devoured by wild beasts. Joseph, the favored son, is now a slave in Egypt. He prospers, but then is imprisoned unjustly and seems to have been forgotten. Then the providential hand of the Lord causes him not only to gain his freedom but also gain a position of honor and power in the Egyptian government. The land surrounding Egypt falls under a great famine, and Joseph's brothers—the ones who sold him—have to come to Egypt, and more specifically to him, for food. It takes a couple of chapters, but there is a reunion. Then their father, Jacob, dies and the brothers fear Joseph's revenge.

Read the encounter with Joseph and his brothers in **Genesis 50:15–21**.

What does Joseph say about his brothers' betrayal and God's plan for his life?

_____

_____

_____

_____

In this story, we get to see what is motivating Joseph's brothers. **Read verse 15**. What do the brothers fear that Joseph will do?

_____

_____

_____

_____

Joseph had relinquished control over his life
and submitted everything to the Lord (verse
19). He had already forgiven his brothers and,
through his relationship with the Lord, had
clearly seen the path that the Lord—not his
brothers—had put him on. Because of Joseph's
belief in the goodness of the Lord, the thought
of revenge—what the brothers think would be
a certainty—isn't even an issue.

Now read **Romans 12:19-21**. Who has the
right to retaliate?

_____

_____

_____

_____

Forgiveness releases you from them, and it releases them into God's hands. You are no longer obligated to perpetuate the hurt that they began. Verse 21 says it all: "Do not be overcome by evil, but overcome evil with good." Don't let what they did overwhelm you; instead, drown the hurt they brought into your life with God's goodness.

From Michelle's Story

"If we don't forgive others, it is impossible for us to heal."

Myth #6: Forgiveness is a process like everything else. I'll forgive eventually, after I've worked through everything. Besides, this offense was really bad, and it's okay not to forgive until I've healed.

You can't heal until you've forgiven. Forgiveness is not the last step of a process; it's the first step that begins a process. Again, consider Jesus and his asking

God to "forgive them for they know not what they do" (Luke 23:34).

When he said this, where was he?

_____

_____

_____

_____

_____

In the course of being the Savior, where was he in the process? When he hung on the cross, was he at the beginning of the process of salvation or at the end? Being crucified was step one to fulfilling all that had been spoken, to actually being the Savior. Forgiveness of those who had betrayed him, beaten him, wrongly accused him, and carried out his sentencing released him to do what he came to do. He could forgive them because he knew that what they were doing was not at all what they thought they were doing. They thought they were killing him, but what they were really doing was launching a grand plan of restoration that would provide them with eternal life.

Myth #7: Forgiveness is weakness. I will not be a doormat ever again. Being too forgiving only gets people hurt. I have to learn to be more assertive.

Read Matthew 5:39–42 written below, and ask yourself, How do you feel about these verses in light of the idea of forgiveness?

"Whoever slaps you on your right cheek, turn the other to him also. If anyone wants to sue you and take your shirt, let him have your coat also. Whoever forces you to go one mile, go with him two. Give to him who asks of you, and do not turn away from him who wants to borrow from you."

Do these verses sound weak to you? Do these verses sound like "doormat" thinking, allowing people to take advantage of you again and again? It's worth considering whether you feel challenged by Jesus' words with the opportunity to be generous with those who have offended you, or if you feel prevented by these words from standing up for your rights. Are you encouraged by what he is asking you to do or are you frustrated?

I think—if honesty rules the day—that we hesitate to forgive because we don't want to be taken advantage of by those who are "enemies" to our hearts. You might be thinking: *These people have hurt us, broken us, and taken from us, and we're supposed to give more?!* I understand completely; I've thought the same thoughts!

Let's also consider something new. Compare Jesus' instructions in the verses in Matthew to Paul's words in Romans 12:21: "overcome evil with good." What do you see as you look at these verses together?

Jesus didn't give instructions that he wasn't ready to illustrate. Look at the story in **John 18:1–11** and **Luke 22:47–53**. Jesus and his disciples are emerging from the inner garden area where he has been praying. Judas steps up to greet him and plants a kiss as a signal that this is the man known as Jesus. The Roman soldiers step up to confirm the identification and ask if he is indeed Jesus. He answers that he is. When the soldiers begin to take Jesus into custody, Peter takes the "not without a fight" stance and he draws a sword and severs the ear of a servant named Malchus. Malchus was one of "them," a slave of the high priest, an enemy. Jesus said, "Stop! No more of this!" He reached down and healed Malchus's ear. Jesus' last healing was for his enemy.

Jesus wasn't anti-assertive. He certainly was assertive with the Pharisees and with the money changers in the temple. In these instances, he was outlining for us exactly how to keep the path clear in our relationship with God. Don't let your feet get all tangled up in the strings of insults and offenses and hurts and betrayals. Take every opportunity to disentangle yourself. Or as Paul would say, "overcome evil with good."

Myth #8: If you don't feel very forgiving when you offer forgiveness, then your forgiveness is false and that's worse than not forgiving at all.

Obedience to the Lord isn't obedience because you feel like being obedient. Obedience is obedience because you obey. Negotiating for exemption is disobedience. Hurt is hurt; but you can hurt *and* obey. You may not understand what happened or why something was done, but you can be confused and still obey.

Let's think about Paul's words to us in his first letter to the Corinthian church. **Read 1 Corinthians 9:24–27**.

I live on a country road and I watch people run and walk in all types of weather: rain, snow, even suffocating heat. I know a few of them. One man jog-walks because he is trying to prevent having another heart attack. There's a young mom who runs because she wants to run a full marathon some day. A high school student endures running the black-topped hills because he wants to win the state cross-country competition this year. When it's raining or hot or frosty, these folks aren't really keen on being outside, but the fruit they hope will come from their workout regimens compels them forward.

Isn't this what Paul is saying in this athletic training illustration? Those who train do so because they want the final outcome, not necessarily because they "feel like it" at the time. The same thing applies to obedience to God. Let the fruit of a right relationship with the Lord compel you to continue your obedience workout to being forgiving. Forgiving when you don't feel like it may seem like running in a thunderstorm or a blizzard. *Why am I doing this?!? This is crazy!!* But the reward of being obedient, pleasing God, and preserving your daily relationship with him is more important than the circumstances.

Has the Lord changed anything about the way you think about forgiveness? In what way? What is your next step in this matter of forgiveness? Be honest and reflect in the space below.

_____

_____

_____

_____

_____

_____

_____

_____

_____

A Thought to Sip On

Forgiveness is God-focused, not offense-focused. The reconciliation that forgiveness brings is between you and God. Distortion of your understanding of forgiveness affects your pure and powerful relationship with the Lord. The issue of unforgiveness is killing your peace, stealing your relationship with the Lord, and eroding your very life.

Discovering the meanings and effects of both forgiveness and unforgiveness may open the door for you to experience a new level of healing in your heart.

If you're not clear on what God actually says about forgiveness, and instead you base your life on a mixture of a smidgen of Bible, a pinch of talk show expert, a dash of reality courtroom drama, and a spoonful of your best friend's mother's opinions, you're in trouble. If your definition and belief about forgiveness is skewed, then your obedience will be hindered.

Forgiveness is an issue that is between you and God. While you have to reconcile with what "they" have done, that reconciling is done with the Lord, not necessarily with "them." If you get to work anything out with "them" directly, that's just icing on the cake. The cake part, the real issue, is constantly staying in the presence of the Lord where he can comfort you, give you understanding, and strengthen you to forgive.

What "they" have done, really, is drive you into God's presence to have real, relevant, relationship-building conversations with him. The path of forgiveness leads straight to the throne of God. And that will always work for your good.

The Great Betrayal

How do you hurt honestly and not hold on to bitterness?

Don't you go thinking, now, that there was no hurt in the Bible! The people God used weren't pretending to hurt or just willing examples for the Bible's authors to write about so that we would have nice "how-to's" on hurting. They hurt. They really, truly hurt. They didn't know how those painful situations they were in would work out. They had the same choice as you have: to choose life or choose death as a result of hurt.

From Michelle's Story

"Still, I hurt. I cried. I couldn't get past my past."

King David was a songwriter, and through his songs we have some great insight into his life. The songs that he wrote are collected in the book of Psalms. A psalm is a song, so the book of Psalms is basically a hymnal. Musical accompaniment would have supported the singers who sang these verses. Through songs, David responds to the events of his life that we read about in the books of Samuel and Chronicles. The psalms that he wrote are a songwriter's journal of his thoughts and feelings: fear, hurt, delight, resignation, and determination.

Songs carry more emotion than chronicles or reports, so if we listen to the music we can hear David's heart intimately. There is one psalm in particular that was written after a deep and treacherous betrayal by someone close. You'll hear the hurt, but then the healing, in David's life.

Read David's song in **Psalm 55**. Listen to it. If you're a musician or just a music appreciator, you can hear the chords change from a minor and echoing description of his pain, through to a full-bodied orchestration of the betrayal and abandonment from his friend, and on to a quiet resolution in a major key to finally a single violin for the last line.

Verse 1: To whom is David addressing his writing?

_____

_____

Verse 2: Describe David's emotional state. What is he feeling? Look for the descriptive words.

_____

_____

_____

_____

Have you ever felt like this when you've been deeply hurt? David says he's in such inner turmoil that he's talking out loud to himself and—as we would say—walking the floor. Have you had those nights of restlessness, flopping around like a fish out of water, replaying the hurtful event over and over and saying what you wish you had said or regretting what you did say?

Verses 4–8: List all the words that describe what David is feeling. Don't miss his true confession, what he feels like doing as a result of all this hurt.

_____

_____

_____

_____

_____

Verses 9–10: What is happening in Jerusalem, "the city"? Who is being affected?

_____

_____

_____

_____

Apparently, whatever hurt David so deeply was also affecting a noteworthy number of people in Jerusalem.

Verse 12–14: Who is causing all this? Look carefully at all the facets of the relationship that David has had with this man?

_____

_____

_____

_____

_____

Verse 15: What does David want to happen to this man and whoever else is with him? (The word *them* indicates more than one person, with this man as their leader.)

_____

_____

_____

_____

Verse 16–17: What is David resolved to do?

_____

_____

_____

_____

Verse 22: What is David going to do with all his hurt?

_____

_____

_____

_____

Cast means to throw something out by hurling or flinging that object away from you. Take the burden, or the offense, whatever it is that "they" have given to you, wad it up and throw it to the Lord. This isn't a game of catch: He'll catch it, but he won't be throwing it back. Once you decide to cast it to him, it's his to do with what he will.

Can you hear the quiet resolution in David's voice at the end of this tempestuous song? *"But I will trust in you."* I can't help but think that with those words, he turns out the light and goes to sleep.

A Thought to Sip On

Hurting when you've been hurt is right. Saying it doesn't hurt when it does or choosing to adopt a pseudo-spirituality that numbs you to pain is unproductive. The Lord knows your heart; he knows you're hurting. You aren't fooling him when you say you aren't. God said that David was a "man after [God's] heart," and yet David hurt. David's friend-turned-foe had hurt many people, deceived them with slick words, and betrayed his friend. There's no indication that God had resolved the problem according to David's request. But David changed in his conversation with the Lord.

The thing about getting to see inside David's heart is that we are not hearing a full report on what happened; we are seeing and feeling a full display of how this event affected his heart. As far as we know, David didn't do anything wrong; he seems to have been blindsided by this hurt. Even though David was God's man, he found himself betrayed, and restless, and distracted by that betrayal. But he addressed his complaint to the Lord, and in a place of intimate fellowship with him, he was able to fully express what he was feeling; his angst over the effects this betrayal, his incredulity that this had come from such a trusted friend, and his silent determination to let all this swirl of hurt rest in the hands of the Lord.

Seventy Times Seven

Let's go straight to **Matthew 18:21–35**.

Jesus tells us about forgiveness. What he shares in this parable resets the parameters of forgiveness then and now. Peter asked the question, resulting in Jesus' telling of the parable. It seemed like such an innocent question. I'm sure Peter felt like he was going to be moved to the front of the class for being so astute. Little did he know that Jesus was about to reveal that what Peter thought was forgiveness and what Jesus thinks are two different thinkings!

From Michelle's Story

"My pain wouldn't heal ... because I had not forgiven."

Read verse 21 and restate Peter's question in your own words.

_____

_____

_____

_____

_____

_____

_____

_____

Jewish tradition and historical rabbinical writings teach that forgiving someone for an offense three times is sufficient. If you want to be especially forgiving, you can add one more, but that's all that you need to do. Does Peter's suggestion intimate that he is beginning to understand the mercy and compassion of Jesus? Maybe; but the point is not Peter's understanding, it is Jesus' answer.

Verse 22: What does Jesus say?

_____

_____

_____

_____

_____

_____

_____

_____

You can either read that number as 77 or as 490 (that's 70 × 7). Either would have shocked the daylights out of all those listening. Jesus is talking to his disciples, so they are familiar with the customs and traditions regarding social interactions. Jesus wasn't being literal here. What he was doing was using a number so far-fetched that it would speak this message to the group: forgiveness has no limit.

Forgiving three times is easy to tally. One offense, two offense, three offense, we're done. But what Jesus said was to forgive people so many times you lose count of how many times you've forgiven them. Forgive them until it becomes a habit. Forgive generously.

Now that he has their collective attention, Jesus shores up this new mandate with a parable to explain.

Let's work out the debt the servant owes the master in the parable. A talent was a lot of money ... a lot! One talent (some translations say "bag of gold") was about twenty years worth of wages for an average laborer. So 10,000 talents would take 200,000 years to repay! Jesus might as well have given the imaginary sum of a gazillion dollars.

Now let's figure out what that servant was owed by his fellow servant. One hundred denarii (or "silver coins") were about twenty weeks' worth of wages. The fellow servant could have paid that back within the year.

Do you see a gross imbalance here? Two hundred thousand years versus twenty weeks!

A gargantuan, unpayable debt that makes 100 denarii look like pocket change.

Read verses 29–30. What does the first servant, who has just been forgiven 10,000 talents, do to his fellow servant who owes him only 100 denarii?

_____

_____

_____

_____

_____

What?! And again I say, *what*?! If the parable ended here, what would you say the meaning of the story or the message of the story was? (This is just a "what-do-you-think" question.) This parable certainly would have raised enough eyebrows to give everybody listening plenty to talk about over dinner that night! Jesus has just blown the doors off of what is considered more-than-good-enough forgiveness practices. But he's not finished yet.

Read verses 31–34. What does the master do as a result of the new information?

_____

_____

_____

_____

_____

Verse 35 is the moral of the story. Write what Jesus says in the space below.

_____

_____

_____

_____

_____

_____

For the sake of repetition and honing in on the most vital issue, how are we told to forgive?

_____

_____

_____

_____

_____

This parable is not about business practices. It's about forgiveness. The Master's generosity is huge. I don't know if we fully comprehend how deep and wide and high and long God's love for us is. While we were still sinning, Paul explains in Romans, Jesus died for us so that our sins could be forgiven (Romans 5:8). That's all of the sins of your lifetime, forgiven: sins in your past and sins in your future that you haven't even conceived of—all forgiven ... all gazillion of them! Are you feeling grateful yet?

At issue in this story is the toll that unforgiveness takes on your life. The first servant seems to be blinded more by the offense from his fellow servant than thankful for the mercy he has received from the master. Jesus, very strategically, reports that the first servant "went out and found" his fellow servant. He didn't just run into him on the street and suddenly remember that his friend owed him money. No, he went looking for him. Not only is he preoccupied with the offense, he is murderously angry about it: he seizes him and chokes him. The first servant seems to be bent on revenge.

What he didn't see coming, and what the listeners to the parable didn't see coming either, is that the one imprisoned and tortured is the one who refuses to extend forgiveness. It's not the one who owes, but the one who won't forgive.

When you are unforgiving, you are the one who ends up tortured. The one who has offended you goes on living, and you end up in torment. The effect is that they've now hurt you twice: once with the original hurt and again with the torment you suffer in your preoccupation and anger.

Forgiveness that comes from the heart, from the seat of your thoughts and feelings, is a recognition of the greatness of God that outweighs the pain of anyone's offense. When your relationship with the Lord is greater than what "they" did, forgiveness is doable.

Celebrate Thanks Living!

God's last straw is our refusal to give thanks.

From Michelle's Story

"Here I was, not enjoying the blessings that Lord had given me with."

The most fundamental definition of thanks is the acknowledgement that somebody did something for you that you didn't do for yourself. Gratitude is like oil in the engine of your spiritual health. It keeps you running smoothly in your relationship with the Lord. Just like we do for our cars, we need to have our thankfulness checked regularly to prevent breakdown. Is that really biblical or just a cute thing to say? Let's see.

Philippians 4:6: "Be anxious for nothing, but in everything by prayer and supplication, with thanksgiving, let your requests be made known to God."

How are the requests that fuel your anxiety to be "made known" to the Lord? According to this verse, what are those two request-making vehicles?

1. _____

2. _____

Prayer is the everyday conversation that we are invited to have with the Lord "without ceasing" (1 Thessalonians 5:17–18). It is part of the normal Christian life, this regular discussion between the heavenly Father and his child. It doesn't require a special posture or a special vocabulary; it's just you and him in relationship. Supplication is a little deeper. It is fervently pleading with the Lord for a desired outcome. This is the asking part of our prayer life. There are other elements of prayer, but these two tend to travel together as a pair, reminding us that healthy prayer consists of both relationship-building conversation and asking.

What accompanies prayer and supplication in Philippians 4:6?

_____

_____

_____

_____

_____

_____

Thanksgiving is the ribbon that wraps the prayer and supplication together. There were any number of great words that Paul could have been directed to write: with honor, with humility, with faith, with confidence. Why do you think Paul said to send your prayer and supplication to the Lord with thanks?

_____

_____

_____

_____

_____

_____

_____

_____

_____

_____

Read Romans 1:21–23. Consider this list to be a progression from a beginning point to an ending point, including all the points in between. There are six points to pass through: from the beginning of a "fall" to hearing the thud at the bottom. Read through these three verses carefully to discover what those six actions are. They are all things that the people described in these verses either didn't do or what they became as a result.

1. _____

2. _____

3. _____

4. _____

5. _____

6. _____

The lack of thanks is part of a downward spiral. Have you ever been on a roller coaster? If you have, then you know it's a risky prospect if you aren't safely strapped into your seat. There are two means of security on every standard roller coaster I've ever ridden on: the seat belt or safety harness, and the bar that you pull into your lap. You want those two things holding you so that you don't spiral off the ride!

Honoring God is like the safety harness and thankfulness is like the bar that comes down into your lap. Those two in combination keep you from spiraling off the ride.

Thought question: How do you see thankfulness and forgiveness working together?

_____

_____

_____

_____

_____

_____

A Thought to Sip On

When forgiveness is a lifestyle, fueled by the consistent practice of thankfulness, you keep your way pure before the Lord. A person's offense has the potential to wound you twice: once in the hurt that it causes and twice by interfering with your relationship with the Lord. As quickly as you would throw down a hot plate, throw unforgiveness far from you by casting it to the Lord. No matter how deep the wound, his love for you is greater still. He wants healing for you, healing that begins when you agree to release the forgiveness that anger and the desire for vengeance have trapped. When you agree with the Lord's mandate to forgive, you have his attention and he hears you. Jesus taught the concept in his model prayer, and then modeled the concept in his life of overcoming evil with good.

God didn't say we would like this forgiveness stuff or embrace it or find it to be easy. He just said to do it. He who knows the heart knows the potential that anger and bitterness and resentment have for destruction when they are bottled up in unforgiveness. Quality of life is what's at stake here—yours!

In one of those songs that King David wrote— Psalm 23—he reveals the key: "You prepare a table before me in the presence of my enemies" (Psalm 23:5). God prepares a table just for you, right in front of your enemies. The table is a gourmet meal, hot and fresh and aromatic, and only set for the two of you. God doesn't chase your enemies away or bring horrible things to punish them for their mistreatment of you. His concern isn't with them; it's with you. You are the guest at his table while they watch. Come to the table. Don't let what they did rob you of your place before him. You matter more.

A Prayer

Great and Mighty Lord, thank you for all that you are in my life.

Thank you for your abounding grace and everlasting faithfulness. May I be as quick to forgive others as you have forgiven me. I beg pardon of everyone, for I have inflicted hurt.

Thank you, Jesus, that I am being freed from the burden I have been carrying for so long of not forgiving others. May bitterness and pain leave my body and may your Holy Spirit fill me with light and let every dark area of my mind be enlightened. May everything I do and say glorify your name.

In Jesus' name, I pray. Amen.

Chapter 3

Steps to Freedom

By Sharon Kay Ball, LPC-MHSP

The loss of a parent in a child's life is incomparable to other losses a child may encounter. There are many reasons for abandonment to occur, yet the void it creates in the child's heart is universal. Sometimes a parent may give their child up for adoption, or a parent may die in a car accident, or other parents, like Michelle's, just walk right out of their child's life.

Our lives are like a puzzle with 1,000 pieces. Each discovery or fact you make in life about yourself is a piece that makes your puzzle picture clearer. The people, life events, or stories about you help define who you are. When key pieces of information about yourself are missing, it creates a void in your heart. These pieces may include unanswered questions: *Why would my mom leave me? Did my dad leave because I was bad? Am I not good enough? Could I have done something different to make them change their mind?*

Another consequence you may experience when abandoned is the lack of basic caretaking in your childhood. This caretaking includes parents providing for their children: food, water, shelter, warmth, a place to sleep, safety from harm, love and belonging, and a healthy sense of self. A parent who really wants to see their child succeed in life will provide an environment that encourages their child to discover their fullest potential for life. The greatest responsibility for parents is sharing with their children the gospel of God's grace and how he loves them more than their parent does.

As you understand what your parent did not provide for you as a child, you will be able to see the loss your parent created when he or she left you. The loss—or missing pieces of your puzzle—varies from situation to situation, yet it leaves you (or any child) with an insecurity that permeates every area of your life. Your foundation of security crumbled when your parent walked out, and you were left to take care of yourself emotionally and physically. When children are abandoned, they learn very quickly not to trust. They learn how to put walls up to protect themselves so they can survive. Your strength of survival is to be admired during your childhood because you stood in the face of many, many unmet needs and challenges and you made it out alive. However, now as an adult, you may want to see more of your life's puzzle complete. In order to do so, you will need to search for some of the "lost" pieces and include "healing" pieces.

Searching for Missing Pieces

Know your loss; it's part of your story. As an adult, you can venture into places of your story that you might not have been able to as a child. God may have protected you by not giving you all the information when you were a child. God allows children to create coping mechanisms to survive what they have gone through. One of those coping mechanisms is "forgetting"—and sometimes you may never remember some of the pieces to your puzzle. As you find yourself in a safer environment, you might remember more parts of your childhood story. Whether you remember your story or not, recognizing what you have lost is key to your journey of healing.

You might want to begin the reflection of your childhood loss with pen and paper. You can start anywhere and in any way you want. This is your story, your reflections. Sometimes it is helpful to begin by writing your first memory before the age of twelve. As you write your memory, try to be mindful of how you feel and what is going on physiologically with you. Do you feel sad, confused, angry, happy, scared, hesitant, or alone? How is your body reacting to this memory? Is your body tense or is your heart racing? Are the palms of your hands sweaty? Do you feel dizzy?

When you are mindful and aware of how you feel and what your body is feeling, you give a gift to yourself by recognizing that this memory is important, whether it is a bad or good one. You are saying to yourself, "I am worth being noticed and loved, and no matter how hard or good this memory may be, I will not leave it. I will attend to it."

Tell your story. Sharing your journey with a friend or counselor gives you a listening ear. Your story is important and you deserve to be heard. During this time you may want to seek professional counseling to support you through this process or find a workbook on grief that will guide you through journaling about the feelings that will arise within your heart.

Grieving the Missing Pieces

Allow yourself to grieve the missing pieces to your puzzle. As you walk through the stages of grief, it is important to know that grief is universal and that it is different for each person. Generally people bounce around the stages of grief. As you move through grief, allow yourself to feel the movement, for where there is movement there is life, and where there is life there is hope. You will make it through, only to find yourself stronger. This is the gift of grief. It acknowledges how deep the loss is, and then gives you strength to handle the depth of loss. Walk gently with yourself through these stages. Be kind, be still, and breathe. You will be amazed when you embrace your grief and no longer fear it. You will see it as your friend and not your enemy.

During these stages, you may not feel Jesus with you, but he is there. He is right there with you. He has never left you. Understanding how it felt when your parent left you may lead you to understand how you have felt left by Jesus. Our view of Jesus is often filtered through our view of our primary caretakers. Our earthly parents do leave, but our heavenly Father does not. It may not feel like it now, but I promise you, he has not left you. Jesus does not force himself upon you; he waits patiently for your calling. Upon hearing your call, he will respond in the ways you need. Maybe right now all you need to know is that he is watching over you, waiting, giving you time to figure out how to start a conversation with him. The time will come to have a conversation with him. That conversation will be part of adding missing pieces to your puzzle.

You might want to start this conversation by making a list of all the questions you have for Jesus. As your list is created, you may find yourself surprised that it parallels the list of questions you have for your parent who left you.

Shock and Denial Puzzle Piece

You may have felt overwhelmed when your parent first left you as a child. You may have gone through a period of shock, and then had to figure out how to move forward in order to survive. Now as an adult, you may also experience a level of shock because you are understanding more of how that abandonment has affected you. At times you may shake your head unable to grasp how your parent could just walk away. There may also be occasions when you have to put that "awareness of abandonment" on a shelf and save it for another day. It might just be too overwhelming to deal with at times.

When you were a child, denial protected you from the flooding of emotions that your little heart could not handle. And at times, denial may still protect you. As an adult, however, you are in a safer place to process these emotions. Trust yourself to see the pain that is actually there. Be gentle. This will be hard and you will feel emotionally and physically exhausted as you process these feelings of abandonment.

Pain and Guilt Puzzle Piece

Pain and guilt may come and go through your journey of healing. As a child you may have felt that it was your fault that your parent left. You may remember times that, as a child, you thought you could have changed the situation "if only" you had done this or that. It is important to know that it was not your fault. There is nothing a child can do to make their parent leave. You are not responsible for your parent leaving. You cannot carry this weight of responsibility anymore. Relinquish it to the person who is responsible for leaving you: your parent.

This might be a good time to write a list of questions you have about why you were abandoned. (You can also refer back to your questions you had for Jesus.) This list of questions has no right or wrong questions. Give yourself the gift of asking all the questions—no restraints. You may not find all the answers, but by asking, you recognize how important the unanswered is to you. This will again reflect your loss.

If you have children, it is sometimes helpful to picture yourself leaving them. Can you do that? Can you picture your little girl or boy with no parent to care for them? More than likely it will bring you to tears to go there. But go there; it will help you connect to that little girl in you that was left. It may even release you from carrying the weight of guilt.

Anger and Sadness Puzzle Piece

You will be angry. You have every right to be angry, whether as a little girl or now a grown woman. You have lost someone in your life that was supposed to be there for you. Try not to hide from your anger. Your anger is there to remind you that it was wrong for your parent to leave you. When you are aware of your anger and are committed to dealing with it in healthy ways, this prevents you from taking your anger out on those around you. Choosing to ignore your anger will only allow it to bottle up inside you and then spew in unhealthy ways on to those you love. This is not helpful to your recovery, nor to those around you. Try to understand and control your anger and find times when you allow your anger to have that voice. Those times could be through writing about it, exercising, or talking with someone.

Sadness is another piece to the puzzle. You may have not realized how deep your sadness is;

once recognized, you are able to make sense of the random tears or confusion within your heart. Your sadness is a reflection of the vast hole that was created in your life when your parent left. This hole is very deep and wide. This depth of sadness may come and go and may have many layers to it. It is okay to weep. It is okay to long for what you didn't have. If you are at work when your sadness hits you and you cannot properly care for it, grab a piece of paper and write a sentence about how you feel in that moment. Take that paper home with you and read it aloud to yourself. Your heart will not forget how it feels and you will be able to attend to your sadness in the way it deserves.

There may be times when you have to walk this part of your grief journey alone. There might be no one in your circle who has experienced pain like this. It may be helpful for you to find a group of women who have experienced the same kind of loss. You can find support groups in your church or community recourses.

Participating in such a group will allow you to be around women who understand this kind of pain. You will feel encouraged and normal by their presence.

Acceptance Puzzle Piece

Through acceptance you recognize the reality of your loss and have found some of the pieces to your puzzle. Acceptance also reminds you that not all puzzle pieces may be found, and yet, you still have the pieces of present and future to add to your puzzle! Acceptance allows feelings of grief to ebb and flow through your life without the feelings of condemnation or shame. It does not mean instant happiness or that all the bad feelings go away. It means you have figured out how to make friends with your grief and move forward, in spite of lacking some pieces to your puzzle. You have figured out how to journey in life, living with emotions that are opposite of each other: joy and sadness. Grief is a combined package of emotions and it takes energy to learn the art of balancing your emotions.

Forgiveness, Another Piece to Your Puzzle

"Everyone says forgiveness is a lovely idea, until they have something to forgive."

—C.S. Lewis

Forgiveness is hard, yet it yields great rewards to you. It may be helpful to start by understanding God's view of forgiveness and many of the obstacles that may prevent you from moving forward and forgiving. You may have thoughts of forgiveness that turn into obstacles, preventing your way to freedom. So let's define what forgiveness is *not*.

- Forgiveness does *not* mean that the person no longer deserves to be punished for the wrong that has been committed against you.

- Forgiveness does *not* mean that you forget the wrong that has been committed against you.

- Forgiveness does *not* mean that you acknowledge the wrong committed against you is okay.

- Forgiveness does *not* mean that you have to give up your righteous anger regarding the wrong committed against you.

- Forgiveness does *not* require you to be in relationship with the person who has harmed you.

Often times the major obstacle to forgiveness is the holding on to your desire to see the person who has sinned against you be punished. By the grace of God we can remove this obstacle by reflecting on how God takes care of that. The apostle Paul writes exactly what God's instructions are regarding your deep desire for revenge: "Never take your own revenge, beloved, but leave room for the wrath of God, for it is written, 'Vengeance is Mine, I will repay,' says the Lord" (Romans 12:19).

God wants you to use your energy to live in peace, which allows you to receive the gift of life rather than the package of bitterness. God sees your painful wounds and will avenge on your behalf, allowing you to focus on forgiving the parent who has left you. In doing this, God is reminding you that he has never left you and he will be with you, bearing the burden of vengeance. He promises to do his job: Revenge is his. Your job: forgive and move forward into life! You have many new pieces to add to your puzzle, and this time you get to choose those pieces. God understands the freedom that comes with forgiveness; that is why this is a command. When you choose to follow his command, you will be free to be a survivor, and not remain a victim.

Forgiveness brings ultimate freedom. God knows that your heart has paid a heavy price by being abandoned. He understands that it is hard to even trust that he will avenge your pain. However, his greatest desire is to see you free and to live the way he created you to live! To forgive the person who hurt you is the grace of freedom. God knew what he was doing when he commanded forgiveness; that is why he took on the part of revenge.

- What are you feeling right now about forgiving your parent who has left you?

- Is it difficult to believe that God will really avenge on behalf of your pain? Why?

- Do you struggle to believe that God will never leave you?

- Do you believe forgiveness is hard? Why?

- Do you believe forgiveness will bring freedom?

- What holds you back from forgiving?

How to Forgive

1. Acknowledge your loss. Only you and God can fully understand the void abandonment left in your heart.

2. In some situations you may be able to express your hurt to your parent in person or by mail.

3. Understand what forgiveness is and what it is not.

4. Put your trust in the role of the Trinity. The design of the Father, Son, and Holy Spirit gives us freedom to forgive:

   • Jesus, the Son of God, showed us how to forgive by dying for our sins.

   • God the Father accepted Jesus' death on our behalf and will avenge your hurt and pain.

- The Holy Spirit gives us strength to do things that are not humanly possible, like forgive those who have left us.

5. Forgive yourself. It is time to let it go. Forgive yourself for holding you responsible for what someone else did. You are not responsible.

6. Give yourself permission to see forgiveness as a daily choice and a gift to yourself. It is exhausting to live in unforgiveness. When we forgive we release ourselves to live fully! Unforgiveness will hold you back.

Forgiveness may need to occur more than once, and that is okay. By giving yourself permission to practice good self-care by attending to your pain, trusting God's role, and practicing forgiveness, you will move from victim to survivor.

As a survivor, your feelings of sadness, disappointment, and anger are familiar territory to you. Though these feelings of hurt may continue to come and go throughout your life, they do not have the same power over you as they did in the past because you have chosen to do the hard work of understanding them. These feelings, caused by your parent who abandoned you, are just a part of your puzzle and story; they no longer define you.

God will give you the gift of strength; accept it. Only he can give you the courage, kindness, and hope that your heart needs to recover from wounds of abandonment.

"We are to forgive so that we may enjoy God's goodness without feeling the weight of anger burning deep within our hearts. Forgiveness does not mean we recant the fact that what happened to us was wrong. Instead, we roll our burdens onto the Lord and allow him to carry them for us."

—Charles Stanley

OTHER BOOKS FROM THE FREEDOM SERIES

When divorce devastates a home, or a woman experiences abuse, paralyzing fear, abandonment, rape, or abortion, she needs God's restoration and wholeness. Michelle Borquez's **FREEDOM series** brings you true stories that show how to heal and experience joy again.

ABUSE TO FAVOR
When abuse happens, as women we tend to take on the pain alone. But you aren't alone and you don't have to deal with it alone. This book helps women understand that it's not your fault and you don't have to face it alone. Paperback, 4.5"x 6.5", 96 pages.

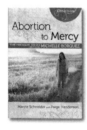

ABORTION TO MERCY
You never thought you would be in the situation of having an abortion and once it's over the pain is still there. But God has not left you because of this one action. This book helps you heal and move past the hurt. Paperback, 4.5"x 6.5", 96 pages.

DIVORCE TO WHOLENESS
Divorce can tear you in half. It's not easy to deal with or sometimes even understand. With *Divorce to Wholeness* you learn how to put yourself back together and become whole again. Paperback, 4.5"x 6.5", 96 pages.

FEAR TO COURAGE

Fear to Courage shows women that they don't have to be a slave to their fears and helps them truly define their fears and develop the courage to move past them. This book shows women that through Christ all things are possible. Paperback, 4.5"x 6.5", 96 pages.

ABANDONMENT TO FORGIVENESS

At some point in every woman's life she has felt a sense of abandonment, for some this feeling is bigger than others. This book teaches women that no matter who has left you, God is always with you. Paperback, 4.5"x 6.5", 96 pages.

DECEIVED TO DELIVERED

She never thought she would cross the line and have an affair, but she did. *Deceived to Delivered* shows women how to strengthen their boundaries and restore their relationships. Paperback, 4.5"x 6.5", 96 pages.